New heart
fresh start

A journey through Lent
for young people

Katie Thompson

Kevin
Mayhew

First published in 1997 by
KEVIN MAYHEW LTD
Rattlesden
Bury St Edmunds
Suffolk IP30 0SZ

0 1 2 3 4 5 6 7 8 9

ISBN 1 84003 103 4
Catalogue No 1500156

Front cover: Paper Collage by Bettina Healey
Cover design by Jaquetta Sergeant
Typesetting by Louise Hill
Printed and bound in Great Britain

Foreword

This book has been written to guide you on a spiritual journey through Lent.

Lent is a time for making peace with ourselves, each other and with God. During this season we are called to 'change our hearts' and find ways to draw closer to God and his love.

New heart – fresh start includes short reflections and prayers based on daily Scripture readings for Lent, with practical suggestions or resolutions for each day. There is a diary at the back of the book so that you can make a record day by day.

I hope you will enjoy using this book throughout Lent, and find a way to make a fresh start and prepare for the joyful celebration of Easter. I hope also that you will begin to know more about a God who is loving and forgiving, and ready to walk beside you not just on your journey through Lent but *every* day, on your journey through life.

KATIE THOMPSON

For Christopher

Ash Wednesday *God will see your goodness*

Reading Jesus said to his disciples, 'Do not show off your goodness for everyone else to see, because it is not others you should want to please, but God. Whatever act of kindness you make, however small it might be, God will always see and return the love you have shown.'
(Based on Matthew 6:1-6, 16-18)

Daily thought It is not *how much* we do that is important to God, but *how* we do it. The smallest act of kindness which is done with a loving and sincere heart means more to God than any dramatic act of goodness which is made without genuine thought or care.

Prayer Lord Jesus,
  during Lent help me to think of others first,
  and put my love into action
  in whatever way I can,
  however small that might be.

Resolution Did you do a good deed for someone today? If you did, write about it in your diary, describing how it made you and the other person feel. If you didn't, think of one you could do tomorrow and write it down.

Thursday after Ash Wednesday　　　　　*'Follow me'*

Reading　　　One day Jesus told his disciples, 'If anyone wants to follow me, they too must carry their own cross with me every day of their lives.'
(Based on Luke 9:23-25)

Daily thought　　Jesus calls each one of us to follow him, but often we find it hard to live up to his expectations of goodness. Jesus understands our difficulties and struggles, and we should remember to ask him to give us the strength to keep on trying.

Prayer　　Lord,
　　help me to feel your love around me always.
In times of trouble help me to know
　　that you are there
　　and your love will always
　　make things right again.
Help me to follow you
　　in spite of any difficulties I might meet
　　on the way.

Resolution　　In your prayers ask Jesus to help you to become more like him. Try writing down some of the ways you feel you could change or improve with his help.

Friday after Ash Wednesday   *Know what is important*

Reading

One day when everyone was supposed to be fasting, the Pharisees and some of the people noticed that Jesus and his disciples were eating as usual. They were annoyed to see that Jewish Law was being disobeyed, and they asked Jesus, 'Why are you eating while everyone else is fasting?'

Jesus answered, 'The friends of the bridegroom would not fast while he is still with them. There will be plenty of time to fast when he has gone.' *(Based on Mark 2:18-22)*

Daily thought

Jesus wanted his disciples to understand that many of the Pharisees paid more attention to their many rules and traditions than to things which were truly important. Jesus gave us two commandments which are more important than any others – to love God and to love our neighbours as ourselves. We must put our love for God and each other before anything else in our lives.

Prayer

Lord, you pour out your love into my life.
Help me to share this love willingly
    with everyone I meet,
    and with you, my heavenly Father.

Resolution

Many people practise some form of fasting during Lent so that they can draw closer to God, taking control of their lives and freeing their hearts to love God more.

There are many different ways of 'fasting' besides giving up food or drink – when you fast with your heart instead of your mouth. This means getting rid of your selfishness and focusing attention on

8

other people and their needs. For example, you could choose to miss a particular television programme and instead share that time with someone who needs help (maybe doing the washing-up or tidying the house). Or you could share that time with someone who simply needs some company – perhaps you have an elderly relative you could spend some time with. If you decide to give up sweets or biscuits, then think about the needs of others and give the money you would have spent to a charity instead.

Everyone can think of something to 'fast' from, so have a go!

Saturday after Ash Wednesday   *Turn over a new leaf*

Reading   One day Jesus noticed a tax-collector called Levi
sitting alone. He said to him, 'Levi, come and follow me.' So Levi got up at once and went with
Jesus.

Later Levi held a party for Jesus and invited
many other tax-collectors to join their celebration.
The Pharisees were outraged to see Jesus eating
and drinking with such dishonest people, but
Jesus said to them, 'People who are well do not
need a doctor, only those who are ill. I have come
to help people like Levi to make a fresh start in
their lives.'
(Based on Luke 5:27-32)

Daily thought   Nobody liked tax-collectors! They were dishonest
cheats who made themselves rich by taking extra
taxes from the people. Jesus forgave Levi and
gave him the chance to give up his dishonest
ways and to 'turn over a new leaf'. Lent is a good
time for us to do the same. None of us is perfect,
and we all make mistakes and do things which
are wrong. Jesus asks each one of us to turn back
to his love, to change our hearts and to try again.

Prayer   Lord Jesus,
help me to make a fresh start this Lent,
to put right what is wrong
and to try to live as Jesus showed me.

Resolution   Just as Jesus gives us the chance to change and
make a fresh start, so we must be ready to do the
same with others. Think of someone who needs to
be given a second chance by you. Remember that

actions often speak louder than words, so tell your diary what you will do to make this person realise that they have a chance to make a fresh start with you. (It could be something as simple as inviting them to join in a game at school.)

First Sunday of Lent   *Don't be tempted*

Reading   Filled with the Holy Spirit, Jesus went into the
                    desert to pray and be close to God.
                        He stayed there for forty days and during that
                    time he had nothing to eat because he was fasting.
                    He looked at the stones around him and knew
                    that he could change them into bread; but he
                    chose not to.
                        As he walked through the desert he knew that
                    he could make himself king over all the land; but
                    he chose not to.
                        When the forty days had passed, Jesus went to
                    the Temple in Jerusalem and climbed the stairs to
                    the rooftop. He knew that if he jumped from the
                    top, God would save him from harm; but he chose
                    not to.
                    (Based on Luke 4:1-13)

Daily thought   Forty days is a long time – almost six full weeks!
                    During the six weeks of Lent we spend some time
                    looking at the good and bad things in our lives.
                    We try to do something for God to show how
                    much we love him. Just as Jesus was tempted to
                    take the easy way out, we too find it hard when
                    we feel tempted to give up, but we must try not
                    to. With God's help Jesus was able to choose to do
                    the right thing and turn away from temptation.
                    With help from our heavenly Father we can do
                    the same! Whether you have chosen to give some-
                    thing up or to do something special during Lent,
                    try to do it every day.

12

Prayer   Lord Jesus, you never gave up
                       even when you found it really difficult.
                     During the six weeks of Lent
                       help me to be strong and to keep my promises
                       as a sign of my love for you.

Resolution   Write down anything special you have chosen to
                     do for Lent. Tell your diary how successful you
                     have been so far (be honest!), and whether you
                     find it easy or difficult.

First Monday of Lent   *Treat others well*

Reading   Jesus told his disciples: One day I will return in
                     glory to sort out the good people from the bad,
                     and I will turn to you and say:
                     　'When I was hungry, you fed me,
                     　when I was thirsty, you gave me a drink,
                     　when you did not know me, you made me
                     　　welcome,
                     　when I had nothing to wear, you gave me clothes,
                     　when I was ill, you took care of me,
                     　when I was alone, you came to visit me.'
                     And you will ask, 'When did I do all these things
                     for you, Lord?'
                     　I tell you whenever you did any of these things
                     for others you did them for me, and because of
                     your goodness you will share in the glory of my
                     kingdom. Those people who turned others away
                     and did not care, did the same to me. On Judgment
                     Day they will be sent away, never to share eternal
                     life with me in heaven.
                     (Based on Matthew 25:31-46)

Daily thought   No one can be good all the time, but we can try to
                     make our loving actions outnumber the unloving
                     ones. When we fill our lives with love and kindness,
                     and try to imagine Jesus in every person we meet,
                     then we will find it easier to treat other people
                     with kindness and respect.

Prayer   Lord Jesus Christ,
                     　watch over and guide me.
                     Help me to remember that
                     　whatever I do to others,
                     　I do to you.

14

Resolution

Try to look for the good points in other people instead of their faults! Choose someone who is not a friend of yours, and try to see the goodness in them. Each of us has our own good and bad points! List in your diary what you think yours are. (See if your family agree!)

First Tuesday of Lent   *Make time for God*

Reading   One day Jesus taught his disciples how to pray to
                    their heavenly Father:
                       Our Father, who art in heaven . . .
                       Then Jesus said, 'Just as you forgive the mistakes
                    that other people make, so your heavenly Father
                    will forgive the mistakes that you make.'
                    (Based on Matthew 6:7-14)

Daily thought   Jesus taught us to think of God as a loving and
                    forgiving 'Father' to all people, who is always ready
                    to listen to our prayers. Praying is like having a
                    conversation with God. We talk to God and he
                    listens, and then, while we listen, God can talk to us
                    too in his own way. Even when we do not know
                    what to say, God can understand our thoughts
                    and feelings without us having to use words.

Prayer   Slowly say the prayer which Jesus taught us, taking
                    time to think about what the words really mean.

Resolution   Close your eyes and listen attentively to the sounds
                    around you. What can you hear? Imagine how
                    different it would be if you did not have the gift
                    of hearing and lived in a world of silence. If we
                    want to hear Jesus speaking to us, then we must
                    remember to sit quietly sometimes and just listen.
                    In your diary, write the sounds that you hear last
                    thing at night or first thing in the morning.

First Wednesday of Lent   *Making choices*

Reading   God said to the prophet Jonah, 'Go to the city of
                     Nineveh and tell the people there that unless they
                     change their wicked ways I will punish them.'
                        So Jonah went to Nineveh and began to preach,
                     'In forty days the Lord will destroy this great city
                     unless you are sorry and change your ways!'
                        The people listened to Jonah and believed what
                     he told them, and they began to pray to God for his
                     forgiveness. God saw that they were truly sorry, so
                     he forgave them and did them no harm.
                     (Based on Jonah 3:1-10)

Daily thought   Even when we turn away from God and get
                     things wrong by making foolish choices, God will
                     always give us another chance to make things
                     right again. Like the people of Nineveh we need
                     to have a change of heart and make a fresh effort
                     to try to be good in the future. When you have to
                     make a choice, stop and think for a moment!
                     Make sure you choose to do what is right, and not
                     just what everyone else does.

Prayer   Lord, when I choose the way to go,
                        help me to choose the good way.
                     When I choose the things to say,
                        help me to say what you'd say.
                     Always help me do what's right,
                        and keep me ever in your sight.

Resolution   Think back over the day. Did you have to make any
                     important choices? Do you feel you made the right
                     ones? Tell your diary about them.

First Thursday of Lent   *God knows best*

Reading   Jesus said, 'Anyone who asks for something will
be answered; anyone who looks will find; and
anyone who knocks will have the door opened.
Just as you want what is good for your children,
how much more does your heavenly Father want
what is good for you!'
(Based on Matthew 7:7-11)

Daily thought   Have you ever prayed for something and then been
disappointed because God did not seem to answer
your prayer in the way you wanted or expected?
God wants us to have anything which brings us
closer to him, but sometimes in our prayers we do
not ask for what is best for us. God knows what our
needs are. As our love and trust for him grows,
we will discover that the things which matter to
us, and for which we pray, are the same things
which are important to God. Every prayer is heard
and answered according to his perfect plan, even
though we might not realise it at the time.

Prayer   Heavenly Father,
you know me so well,
and you take care of all my needs.
May my prayers always draw me
closer to your love.

Resolution   It is important to pray for the needs of other people
as well as your own. Select a prayer from a book,
or one which you know well, and say that prayer
especially for someone you choose. Write their
name or names in your diary, and the reasons why
they need your prayers.

First Friday of Lent   *Make peace*

Reading   Jesus said, 'If you are about to come before God to
                     pray, and then remember that you have quarrelled
                     with someone, first go away, settle your argument
                     and make your peace with them.'
                     (Based on Matthew 5:23-26)

Daily thought   If we have done something to spoil our friendship
                     with another person, then we have spoiled our
                     friendship with God too. Sometimes feelings of
                     anger and hurt get in the way of love and kindness.
                     When we forgive someone, or they forgive us, then
                     we lose these bad feelings and they are replaced
                     by happiness and peace.

Prayer   Lord, if I have hurt anyone
                         by what I have said or done,
                         if I have ignored someone
                         or made them feel unloved,
                         if I have been unforgiving, and full of anger,
                         then I am truly sorry
                         and ask for your forgiveness.

Resolution   It is good to tell God that we are sorry and that we
                     love him for forgiving our sins. Write your own
                     prayer telling God all these things.

First Saturday of Lent   *Love everyone*

Reading   One day Jesus said, 'If someone hits you, do not
                     hit them back; instead you must forgive them and
                     try to be their friend. Learn to love your enemies
                     and to pray for anyone who wishes you harm. It
                     is easy to love someone who loves you back, but
                     it is hard to love someone who hurts you. Try to
                     be like God the Father who always forgives. If
                     you do this, others will see God's goodness in you,
                     and my Father in heaven will be very pleased.'
                     (Based on Matthew 5:43-48)

Daily thought   We all find it hard to love someone who does not
                     love us in return or makes our life difficult.
                     However, Jesus asks us to forgive anyone who has
                     hurt us, even when that might seem impossible! If
                     we allow Jesus to share *his* love with *us*, then we
                     will find it easier to love as he loves and to forgive
                     as he forgives.

Prayer   Even as Jesus was hanging on the cross,
                        he forgave the soldiers who crucified him.
                     Help me to forgive anyone who has hurt me,
                        and never to harm anyone
                        by my words or actions.

Resolution   If you have quarrelled with someone or they have
                     upset you, write down what you can do about it.

Second Sunday of Lent   *God's glory*

Reading   One day Jesus asked Peter, James and John to come and pray with him. He led them to the top of a steep mountain, where it was peaceful and quiet, and they could be alone. Jesus began to pray to his heavenly Father when suddenly he appeared to change! His face and clothes shone with a brilliant light, as dazzling as the rays of the sun. Then the disciples saw Moses and Elijah on either side of Jesus, talking to him. Peter jumped up with excitement and said, 'Lord this is wonderful! I could make three shelters – one for each of you!'

At that moment a cloud streaming with light appeared above them, and a voice said, 'This is my Son whom I love very much. Listen to what he says.'

The disciples were so terrified that they threw themselves to the ground and hid their faces. Then Jesus said gently, 'Get up, my friends, do not be afraid,' and looking up they saw that Jesus was standing alone.

(Based on Matthew 17:1-8)

Daily thought   The light shining from Jesus was as bright as the sun. Those rays of light were shafts of God's glory and a glimpse of his power and might. We cannot look directly at the sun because its brightness is too powerful for our eyes, but we see its light reflected off the things around us. We cannot touch sunlight, but we can feel the warmth of its rays. So it is with God! We cannot see or touch him directly, but we see his glory reflected in the whole of creation and feel the warmth of his love in our everyday lives.

Prayer   Lord God,
               help me to see your glory
               in the world around me,
               and to feel the warmth of your love
               which shines on every living thing.

Resolution   It isn't easy to be a shining example of God's
               goodness! Do you think that other people see the
               reflection of God's love in you? In your diary,
               make a list of any people that you feel are 'shining
               examples' for us all. It might be someone famous
               like Mother Teresa, or someone you know person-
               ally. Write down the qualities which you feel make
               them special people.

Second Monday of Lent   *Be fair*

Reading   Jesus said, 'Be loving, just as your heavenly Father
                     is always loving. Do not believe that you are always
                     right and others are wrong, but treat everyone the
                     way you would want to be treated yourself. If
                     you are forgiving with others, then God will be
                     forgiving with you.'
                     (Based on Luke 6:36-38)

Daily thought   Jesus wants us to love other people as freely and
                     generously as he does. By our actions we will
                     become more and more like him. Although we
                     won't always find it easy, if we allow him to,
                     God's spirit will help us. We must learn that we
                     need to forgive and to be forgiven to experience
                     true happiness. Jesus will give us the strength to
                     make our peace with each other.

Prayer   Lord, teach me to be fair,
                         to be ready to listen to others
                         and to accept the times
                         when they are right and I am wrong.
                     Help me to forgive others,
                         just as I know you will always forgive me.

Resolution   How many times should you be ready to forgive
                     someone? You might feel that your answer would
                     depend on what they have done and how many
                     times they have done something wrong. Read what
                     Jesus tells us in Matthew 18:21-22. There are many
                     different ways of saying sorry and making peace!
                     Write some suggestions of things you would do
                     to show someone that you had forgiven them and
                     wanted to be friends again.

Second Tuesday of Lent   *Practise what you preach*

Reading   Jesus said to the crowds, 'Listen to what the Pharisees tell you and do what they say, but do not copy what they do. They do not put their words into action or practise what they preach. They are full of self-importance and pride, and you must not follow their example. It is God that is important and you must be ready to serve him and one another.'
(Based on Matthew 23:1-12)

Daily thought   We are all very good at telling other people what *they* should do, but often we aren't very good at actually doing it ourselves – we don't 'practice what we preach'. Jesus wanted us to understand that it is important for us to put our words into action, and to show how much we care for each other by what we *do* and not just what we say.

Prayer   Lord Jesus,
   help me to make my actions
   speak louder than words,
   and to follow your loving example.

Resolution   Think of something you can do to show someone that you care about them (for example, do the washing-up, tidy your bedroom, give them a hug), and then make sure you do it. Tell your diary what happened and how it made you and them feel.

Second Wednesday of Lent   *A place in heaven*

Reading   The mother of the two disciples James and John came to Jesus and asked him, 'Master, can my sons sit on either side of your throne in the kingdom of heaven?'

Jesus answered, 'Only my heavenly Father can decide this.'

When the other disciples heard what had happened, they were angry and began to quarrel amongst themselves.

Jesus told them, 'You must not argue about which of you is the greatest! Remember I have come as a servant and not as a king, and only by serving others and putting them before yourselves will you be considered great in my Father's kingdom!' *(Based on Matthew 20:17-28)*

Daily thought   God measures greatness by how good and willing we are to think of others before ourselves. Jesus came to serve everyone and put our needs before his own by dying on the cross to save us from sin. By being unselfish and generous with our love we can be sure of a place with Jesus in heaven.

Prayer   Jesus,
        teach me to be loving and caring,
        and to think of others
        before thinking of myself.

Resolution   Remember the words of Jesus: 'Whatever you do to others, you do to me'. Think back over the day, and write about an act of kindness you were able to do, or which you saw someone else do.

Second Thursday of Lent   *Lazarus and the rich man*

Reading

One day Jesus told this story: Once there was a rich man who had fine clothes and the best of everything that money could buy. He spent his time enjoying himself and feasting with his rich friends.

On the street outside his house lay a poor man called Lazarus who was thin and hungry, and covered in sores. Lazarus would gladly have eaten the rich man's scraps if they had been offered to him.

Lazarus died and went to heaven where he was truly happy at last. When the rich man died he went to hell and, seeing Lazarus so happy, he cried out to him for help. But God asked the rich man, 'Did you help when Lazarus cried out for food? Did you care for him when he was ill and had nowhere to go? You thought only of yourself, and gave up the chance of everlasting happiness with me.'

(Based on Luke 16:19-31)

Daily thought

In this story Jesus wanted to show us that being well off and comfortable can make us 'blind' to the needs of people around us. We can become selfish and self-centred, caring only about our own happiness. Sadly there are many homeless and poor people in our world today, who feel unloved and abandoned just as Lazarus did. Sometimes we have the opportunity to help such people in our own neighbourhood, but we should always treat them with compassion and respect, and remember to keep them in our prayers.

26

Prayer   Lord, sometimes I take what I have for granted.
I grumble and complain,
    and wish that I had even more.
Help me in my own way, however small,
    to act generously whenever I can.

Resolution   Say a prayer for the homeless and poor everywhere,
and for all the people who do so much to help
them and restore their hope. Perhaps you could
organise a Lenten collection of food or blankets
which could be donated to a local refuge for the
homeless. Write down your ideas and any people
who might be willing to help you (for example,
teachers at school).

Second Friday of Lent   *Listen to God's message*

Reading Jesus told another parable to the people: There was once a farmer who owned a vineyard. He had to go away on business, and so he put some farm workers in charge of the vineyard. When it was time to harvest the grapes, the farmer sent some servants to collect his share. But the farm workers beat his servants and chased them away. The farmer did not give up and sent more servants to collect what belonged to him. Again they were beaten and chased off. Finally the farmer sent his own son.

'I am sure that they will treat him better,' he said.

Instead the farm workers seized the son and killed him.

Then Jesus asked, 'What will the farmer do when he arrives at the vineyard?'

The people who had been listening answered, 'He will punish the farm workers and put other people in charge of the vineyard.'
(Based on Matthew 21:33-43)

Daily thought Imagine if the vineyard was the whole world. Who would be in charge of it all? God made the world, and everything in it belongs to him. In the story he is like the farmer; he trusts us to take care of all that we have been given, just as the farmer trusted the farm workers. God sent his only Son Jesus to carry his message, just as the farmer in the story sent his son. Many people listened and trusted in this message of love, but some turned away and, in time, had Jesus put to death. Just as the vineyard was taken away from the farm workers who would not listen to their master's message, so the kingdom of God will be taken from those who do not listen to God's message and given to others who can be trusted to listen and live according to God's way. We must be ready to listen to God's word if we want to share in his kingdom of love.

Prayer

Jesus, open my ears to hear your message,
   and help me to share the message
   of your saving love with others,
   so that they too can share
   in your heavenly kingdom.

Resolution

Jesus used parables to explain his message in a way we could understand and remember. Think of a parable you can remember, and in your own words write what you think it teaches you. Can you find the story in your Bible?

Second Saturday of Lent *The son who came back*

Reading

One day Jesus told this story: There was a man who had two sons and the younger one came to his father and said, 'Father give me everything that will one day belong to me, so I can enjoy my riches now.'

The father did this and the younger son set off to look for adventure. He travelled to a distant land and spent all his money enjoying himself.

There was a famine in that land, and the young man found himself penniless and hungry. 'If I stay here I will surely starve,' he thought, so he decided to return to his father and ask for his forgiveness.

The father saw his son coming and ran to welcome him. As he hugged him, the young man said, 'Father I am so sorry. I no longer deserve to be called your son.' But his father told his servant to prepare a feast and to bring the finest clothes, and they began to celebrate.

(Based on Luke 15:11-24)

Daily thought

Jesus told this story because he wanted us to understand that, whatever we do wrong, we can always come back to our heavenly Father to ask for his forgiveness, knowing that he will welcome us back with open arms. God's love is unconditional; it does not change according to whether we have been good or bad. His love for us is so great that, no matter what we might have done, he will wait patiently and welcome us with joy when we return to him.

30

Prayer

Lord Jesus,
    by spending time
    with the tax-collectors and sinners,
    you showed me how much
    our heavenly Father loves *all* of us.
If I have turned away
    from God's friendship and love,
    help me to turn back to him
    full of confidence and trust.

Resolution

Try to remember some of the stories Jesus told, or things that he did, to show us how loving and forgiving our heavenly Father is. Write down what you can think of in your diary. If you want to, look up and read Luke 7:36-50. Was this story on your list?

Third Sunday of Lent   *The water of life*

Reading   Jesus had been walking all morning and was tired
                   and thirsty. He had stopped to rest beside a well
                   when a Samaritan woman came to fill her water
                   jug. Jesus asked her, 'Will you give me a drink?'
                   The woman was surprised because Jews and
                   Samaritans usually hated each other and rarely
                   spoke.
                       'Surely, sir, you are a Jew. Why should I share
                   my water with you?'
                       Jesus answered, 'If you knew me, it would be
                   you asking me for a drink, for I would give you
                   the water of life.'
                       The woman was puzzled, 'The well is deep and
                   you have no bucket, so how could you reach this
                   "living water"?'
                       Jesus said, 'When you drink the water from this
                   well, your thirst always returns. Anyone who
                   drinks the water that I can give will never be thirsty
                   again. This water will become a spring inside them
                   and fill them with eternal life.'
                       The woman said to him, 'Sir, share this water
                   with me.'
                       Then Jesus told the woman many things about
                   herself that no other person knew, and she believed
                   that he was indeed the Son of God. When she told
                   the people of the town what had happened at the
                   well, they too believed in Jesus.
                   (Based on John 4:6-11, 13-19, 28-29, 39-42)

Daily thought Just spend a few moments thinking about how
                   many times today you have used water! How dif-
                   ferent our lives would be if water was scarce or
                   had to be collected with a bucket from a well. Water
                   is a symbol or sign of life; without it everything

32

would die. Jesus is the 'water of life' who fills us with his love and goodness so that we can have everlasting life.

Prayer

Thank you, Lord Jesus,
  for the rain and the rivers,
  and the mighty oceans,
  for being able to turn on a tap
  and know that water will flow.
Thank you for the 'water of life',
  so generously poured out and shared with me.
Help me to pour out that love on others.

Resolution

Are the following statements true or false?

1 More than 70 per cent of the earth's surface is covered by water.
2 Water freezes at 5°C.
3 More than two thirds of the human body is made of water.
4 Water can be a liquid, gas or solid.
5 Water boils at 120°C.

Think back over the day and try to remember how many times you used water today! Make sure that tomorrow you use it carefully and without wasting it, remembering people elsewhere in the world who are not so fortunate! Every time you use water tomorrow, give thanks to God silently in your heart.

Third Monday of Lent   *The power of God's word*

Reading   The king of Syria had an army commander called
                     Naaman who suffered from leprosy. Naaman heard
                     that the prophet Elisha, who lived in Israel, might
                     be able to cure his leprosy, so he asked for the
                     king's permission to travel to Israel and find him.
                     The king agreed, and Naaman set off in his chariot
                     to ask for Elisha's help.

                     'Go to the river Jordan and bathe there seven
                     times,' Elisha told him, but Naaman refused to
                     believe that simply washing in the river would
                     cure him, and he stormed off in a rage. Eventually
                     Naaman's servants convinced him that it could
                     do no harm to try something so simple, and
                     Naaman bathed in the river just as Elisha had told
                     him. When he emerged from the water, he was
                     amazed to find that his leprosy had gone and he
                     was completely cured.

                     Naaman returned to thank Elisha and said to
                     him, 'Now I know that the God of Israel is indeed
                     the one true God.'
                     (Based on 2 Kings 5:1-15)

Daily thought   We can all be like Naaman sometimes – too proud
                     and stubborn to listen to others and unwilling to
                     take their advice. Naaman expected some sensa-
                     tional, dramatic act of healing from Elisha, and was
                     disappointed to be told simply to wash in the river.

                     God does not need to prove himself by dra-
                     matic gestures – his word is all-powerful even if it
                     is sometimes quiet and simple. God speaks to us
                     too, in prayer, in the scriptures and through the
                     people around us. His power can work in our
                     lives if we are not too proud and independent to
                     listen and respond.

34

Prayer   God our Father,
                      just as Naaman had a change of heart,
                      and was ready to listen
                      and respond to your word,
                      help me to do the same,
                      so that the power of your word
                      can work in my life too.

Resolution   When someone talks to you, be ready to listen
                      carefully to their words. Give them your individual
                      attention and sit quietly so that you can hear what
                      they are saying. Tell your diary whom you particu-
                      larly enjoy listening to and why.

Third Tuesday of Lent   *Keep on forgiving*

Reading   One day Jesus told a story about a king who had
many servants. One servant owed the king a great
deal of money, but he had nothing to pay him with.
'I will sell you and your family as slaves, and
use the money to pay off your debts,' said the king.
The servant fell to his knees and begged for
another chance. 'Somehow I will repay everything
I owe,' he pleaded. The King was a kind and generous man and, taking pity on the servant, cancelled
his debts and let him go.
Later that day the servant met another man who
owed him a small amount of money. When he
could not pay what he owed, the servant had him
thrown into jail.
When the news reached the king, he sent for
the unforgiving servant. 'Could you not forgive
someone as I forgave you?' he asked. Then he had
the servant thrown into prison until he could pay
back everything he owed.
Jesus said, 'Just as my Father forgives you, so
you must be ready to forgive others with all your
heart.'
(Based on Matthew 18:23-35)

Daily thought   All of us find it very difficult to forgive someone
who has wronged us, but that is what Jesus asks
us to do. We must try to forgive, and hope that such
a person will change, and become more aware of
the unhappiness they have caused by their actions.
Jesus understands that we do not find this easy,
but with his love and help we can move slowly
towards forgiving our 'enemies' and, in doing so,
we will know forgiveness ourselves.

Prayer   Lord Jesus,
                      help me turn anger into love
                      and to forget any grudges that I bear.
                  Forgive me
                      just as I am ready to forgive others.

Resolution   Design a poster to encourage forgiveness and peace.
                  It could refer to your own local school or neigh-
                  bourhood, or concern our world in general.

Third Wednesday of Lent   *God's rules*

Reading   Jesus said to the crowds who had gathered to listen
                  to him, 'I have not come to change the command-
                  ments, but to make them complete. They tell us
                  what we should and should not do if we are to live
                  in God's way. Whoever keeps God's command-
                  ments and teaches others to do the same, will be
                  considered truly great in my Father's kingdom.'
                  (Based on Matthew 5:17-19)

Daily thought Imagine what would happen if everyone decided
                  to make up their own rules of the road – traffic
                  lights and speed limits would be ignored, and chaos
                  and confusion would soon follow. Abandoning
                  rules and regulations would quickly make it
                  impossible to drive safely on the roads. Rules are
                  made to make something work successfully, and
                  to allow us freedom while keeping us from harm.
                  God's rules help us to know and love him, and
                  allow us the freedom to lead lives filled with
                  goodness and love, teaching us to do good, both
                  for ourselves and our neighbours.

Prayer   Heavenly Father,
                  help me to live by your rules of love,
                  and to share them with other people.

Resolution   Below are the Ten Commandments given to Moses
                  by God. (If you want, you can read about this in
                  the Book of Exodus, chapter 20.) They have been
                  jumbled up and written in the wrong order. Can
                  you put them in the right order, numbering them
                  1 to 10? (Even adults might find this one tricky!)

- Do not kill anyone.
- Do not steal or take what does not belong to you.
- There is only one God; put nothing else before him.
- Do not use God's name unnecessarily.
- Be faithful to the one you married.
- Love and respect your parents.
- Remember the greatness and mystery of God.
- Make Sunday God's special day of worship.
- Don't be jealous or envious of anything which belongs to other people.
- Tell the truth about other people.

Third Thursday of Lent   *Listen to God's call*

Reading   God promised the Israelites that, if they obeyed his
                      Commandments, he would be their God and they
                      would be his people. Despite his love and care for
                      them, they chose to turn away from him. They
                      disobeyed his commandments and became more
                      selfish and unkind.
                         God said to Jeremiah, 'I have sent many messen-
                      gers like you to call my people back to me, but they
                      refuse to listen, and they will not answer my call.'
                      (Based on Jeremiah 7:23-28)

Daily thought   Often we are like the Israelites when we choose to
                      turn away from God and ignore his call. Sometimes
                      it is simply easier to do what *we* want to do, rather
                      than what God expects or asks us to do. Why
                      should we put ourselves out to do something for
                      someone, when we would much rather play foot-
                      ball or go out with our friends. However much
                      we ignore God, he is always ready to welcome us
                      back when we turn to him and say sorry, because
                      he is our heavenly Father and we are his children.

Prayer   Lord, help me to grow closer to you,
                          so that when you call
                          I will hear and answer you.

Resolution   Set aside some time to talk to God. It could be on
                      your way to school, while you brush your teeth,
                      before you go to bed – but make it a special time
                      when you can be quiet and on your own with
                      God. Tell your diary when you plan to do this and
                      whether you found it easy or difficult.

Third Friday of Lent   *The greatest Commandments*

Reading   One of the scribes came to Jesus and asked, 'Which of the commandments is the most important?'

Jesus answered, 'To love God with all your heart, and all your mind and all your strength, and to love others as much as you love yourself. These commandments come before all others!'

Then the scribe said to Jesus, 'What you have said is true, because nothing is more important than loving God and loving our neighbours.'

Seeing that the scribe was wise and good, Jesus said to him, 'My friend, what you have said will please God and keep you close to him.'
(Based on Mark 12:28-34)

Daily thought   Our neighbours are not just the people we know well, our friends and those we like. They include the people we meet by chance every day of our lives – each one of these is a neighbour. Jesus showed us *how* to love God and our neighbour. He puts his words of love into action every day, and this is what he asks us to do too. St Paul wrote a letter to the Christians who lived in the Greek city of Corinth, to remind them of the perfect love which Jesus had shared with everyone:

Love never hurries; it is always kind.
It is not jealous,
    and never boasts of its greatness.
Love is never rude or selfish.
It is always ready to forgive
    and forget mistakes that we make.
Love is no friend of wickedness,
    but delights in honesty and truth.
Love is strong and never gives up.

It never loses trust in God
   or its hope for the future.
Love will survive all things
   because it is everlasting.
(Based on 1 Corinthians 13:4-7)

Prayer

Lord,
   I have only one life,
   and shall not live this day again.
Help me to remember
   that everyone is my neighbour.
If I can do something good
   or show my kindness,
   then let me do it today,
   for unless love is shared it cannot grow.

Resolution

Think of the people who love and care for you every day – at home, at school or in your neighbourhood. Think of anyone who needs *your* love. How can you show them that you care? Write some ideas in your diary.

Third Saturday of Lent   *The Pharisee and the tax-collector*

Reading   One day Jesus told this parable. Two men went to the temple to pray. One was a Pharisee who was an upright and religious man who always obeyed the law. The other was a tax-collector who cheated people to make himself rich.

The Pharisee stood up and prayed aloud, 'Thank you God for making me such a good person, unlike the tax-collector over there! I keep all your rules and am most generous with my money.'

The tax-collector stood at the back of the temple. He bowed his head in shame as he prayed quietly, 'O God, I have done so many things wrong, please forgive me.'

Jesus said, 'It was the second man, and not the first, who pleased God with his prayer.'
(Based on Luke 18:10-14)

Daily thought   The Pharisees were proud of their 'goodness' and thought that they were closer to God than anyone else. Jesus is not impressed by outward gestures of goodness; what matters to him is what we feel in our hearts. The Pharisee was proud and full of self-importance, and so busy parading his good deeds that he pushed God to one side and forgot that everyone needs God's forgiveness and mercy. The tax-collector knew that he was far from perfect, and just how much he needed to be forgiven. We all worry too much sometimes about what others think about us, and allow pride to come between ourselves and God. No one is perfect, and every one of us needs to ask for God's love and mercy.

Prayer

Lord Jesus,
   look into my heart and see my love for you.
Help me to be humble and to admit my mistakes,
   knowing that I can always turn to you
   and ask for your forgiveness

Resolution

It is hard to admit when we are wrong, but it is important to look at our mistakes if we are to put them right. Spend some time thinking about any things you have done wrong or mistakes you have made recently. Write a prayer telling God you are sorry and asking him to help you to be good.

Fourth Sunday of Lent — *The Light of the World*

Reading

As Jesus walked along one day, he passed a beggar who had been blind since birth. He turned and said to his disciples, 'I am the Light of the World,' before bending down to mix some spittle and dust into a muddy paste. He smeared this paste on the eyes of the blind man, and told him to go and wash them in a nearby pool. The man did what Jesus had told him, and was amazed to find that he could see!

When the crowds heard what Jesus had done, they took the beggar to the religious leaders and told them what had happened. At first they would not believe the beggar and asked, 'Who was this man who made you see?'

The beggar replied. 'He was a prophet from God!'

The people were outraged, 'A holy man would never do such a thing on the Sabbath!' they exclaimed.

But the beggar persisted, 'I was blind, and this man made me see, surely he could not have done such a marvellous thing unless he had been sent by God!'

The Pharisees were furious and had the beggar sent away.

Later Jesus came to find the beggar and asked him, 'Do you believe in the Son of God?'

'Show him to me, sir, and I will believe,' replied the beggar.

Then Jesus said gently, 'He is speaking to you.' The beggar fell to his knees and said, 'Lord, I believe in you!'

(Based on John 9:1-38)

Daily thought Jesus, the 'Light of the World', brought light into the blind beggar's life by making him see and allowing him to recognise Jesus as the Son of God. Sometimes we are 'blind' and fail to 'see' God's goodness in the people and in the world around us. We need Jesus to open our eyes of faith so that we can know and recognise him just as the beggar did.

Prayer Dear Jesus,
   thank you for the gift of sight,
   which allows me to see
   the beauty of your world.
Open my eyes
   so that I can look and find your goodness
   everywhere I go
   and in everyone I meet.

Resolution While someone is around to make sure you are safe, try wearing a blindfold for an hour. Can you imagine what a great gift Jesus gave to the beggar when he restored his sight? Write down what you found most difficult when you were wearing the blindfold!

Fourth Monday of Lent   *Have faith*

Reading   Jesus went to a town called Cana, in Galilee, and
while he was there a royal official, whose son was
dying, came to ask Jesus for his help. Jesus said to
him, 'Must I perform miracles to make you believe?'
   But the official insisted, 'Sir, please come, or my
son will surely die!'
   'Go home,' said Jesus, 'and your son will live.'
   The royal official trusted Jesus, and set off for
home at once. On the way some of his servants
met him and told him with great excitement how
his son had miraculously recovered! The official
told them everything that had happened, and
they too believed in Jesus.
(Based on John 4:46-54)

Daily thought   Sometimes it is hard to believe that something is
true unless we have some proof; otherwise we
feel full of doubt and uncertainty. The disciple
called Thomas would not believe that Jesus had
risen from the dead without seeing his wounds
for himself. Jesus understood that like Thomas
many would be filled with such doubt. Some
people, like the royal official, have remarkable
faith in Jesus and the power of his word, and are
ready to put complete trust and confidence in
God. However, most of us are more like doubting
Thomas, and must ask for God's help to make our
faith grow stronger.

Prayer   O Lord, please stand beside me,
         and walk with me each day.
   With you to lead and guide me,
         I'm sure to find the way.

At times my faith will falter
and I will feel unsure,
but I need not be frightened
for your love will endure.

Resolution Choose one of the biblical stories below which tell about other people who had remarkable faith in God.

1. Genesis 22:1-13

2. Luke 7:1-10

3. Matthew 15:21-28

4. Mark 5:25-34

Tick which one you chose, and describe what happens.

Fourth Tuesday of Lent   *The paralysed man*

Reading   While Jesus was in Jerusalem, he came across a
poor man who had been paralysed for many
years. The man lay uncared for among a crowd of
sick and handicapped people who gathered around
a pool called Bethesda. (These people believed
that when the water was disturbed by one of God's
angels, the first person to bathe in the pool would
be cured of their illness.)

Jesus asked the paralysed man, 'Do you want
to be well again?'

'Yes, sir,' he replied, 'but no one will help me to
the water in time and I always miss my chance.'

Then Jesus said to him, 'Pick up your mat and
walk.' The man was able to pick up his mat and
walk away.

All of this took place on the Sabbath day, and
when the people saw the man carrying his mat,
they were furious. He explained what had happened but could not tell them the name of the
kind stranger who had cured him. Later, when the
religious leaders discovered that it was Jesus who
had cured the paralysed man on the Sabbath, they
began to make their plans against him.

(Based on John 5:1-16)

Daily thought   The Sabbath was, and still is, a strict day of prayer
and rest, when work of any kind is against the
Jewish Law. Jesus acted out of love and pity for
the poor man who lay paralysed and uncared for.
He wanted the people to understand that rules
and laws should not stop them from acting with
kindness and love. The two greatest commandments Jesus gave us are to love God and to love
each other. Jesus chose to help the paralysed man

on the Sabbath day, and showed us that if we choose to put God's rules of love first, then we will always do what is right.

Prayer

Heavenly Father,
please help me
to make the right decisions in life,
so that I always choose to do your will,
and lead a life full of love and kindness.

Resolution

Write down the rules which play a part in your life. (They could be rules in school or at home.) Are they God's rules or man-made rules? Do any of them get in the way of God's love?

50

Fourth Wednesday of Lent

*'Believe in me and
the one who sent me'*

Reading   Jesus said to the Pharisees, 'Just as the Father can give life to the dead, so too can the Son give life to whoever he chooses. Anyone who does not believe in the Son does not believe in the Father who sent him. Whoever listens to me and believes in the Father who sent me truly has eternal life.'
(Based on John 5:19-24)

Daily thought   God the Father sent his only Son Jesus to rescue us from our sins and lead us back to his love. Jesus is one with his Father, and who better to teach us about God's love and how to live so that he can give us eternal life? If we grow close to Jesus, by our thoughts and actions, then we also grow close to our heavenly Father.

Prayer   Lord,
please help me to listen to your word,
so that I might know
and understand your way,
and grow ever closer to you.

Resolution   Spend some time getting to know God better by reading John 3:16-21. What can you learn from Jesus about the way God wants you to live? Write your thoughts in your diary.

Fourth Thursday of Lent *'I have the message of eternal life'*

Reading Jesus said to the Pharisees, 'You sent messengers to John the Baptist to ask him who I was. Now I tell you that I have been sent by my heavenly Father and everything I do is done through him. You believe that the scriptures can show you the way to everlasting life, yet even when they bear witness to me, you will not believe in the very one who has come to share that eternal life with you.'
(Based on John 5:33, 36, 39-40)

Daily thought Have you ever heard the expression, 'You can't see the wood for the trees'? Do you understand what it means? Even when something is really obvious, and we are surrounded by what we need to see or know, we still manage to miss the point. The Pharisees looked to the scriptures to tell them about the promised Messiah, but even when all the prophesies pointed clearly towards Jesus, they still failed to recognise him as the Son of God. Sometimes we too fail to recognise Jesus in the world around us, and are 'blind' to his goodness in other people.

Prayer Lord Jesus,
　　you are the Word of God
　　and you have the message of eternal life.
　Open my ears to hear your message
　　and lead me to everlasting happiness.

Resolution Think back over the events of the day or the past week and try to remember any occasion when Jesus was present and working through someone, even though you might not have recognised him at the time. It could be someone who did a good deed or treated you kindly. Write it down and tell your diary what happened.

Fourth Friday of Lent   *'I come from the one who sent me'*

Reading   Many of the religious leaders wanted to have
Jesus killed, so he travelled to Jerusalem without
drawing unnecessary attention to himself. The
people there were uncertain about whether or not
Jesus was indeed the Christ, so he said to them,
'You believe that you know where I come from,
but you do not know the one who sent me, but I
know him and come from him.'
  They would have arrested him there and then,
but the time was not right and they left him alone.
(Based on John 7:1-2, 10, 25-30)

Daily thought   It is impossible for us to understand all about
God – the mystery of three persons in the Holy
Trinity, someone who has no beginning and no
end! We do not need to worry about understanding,
we just need to have faith in God's power and
love. Jesus was sent to lead us to know God the
Father through his words and actions. By knowing Jesus we learn so much about a God who is
loving and forgiving and wants us to be happy.

Prayer   Lord Jesus,
    help me to know you better,
    to listen to your words,
    and think about your message of love,
    so that I too may know the one who sent you.

Resolution   Our knowledge of God is nourished by his word
which we find in the Bible. The Bible is rather like
a library of writings, history, stories, poetry and
letters. All, in their own way, reveal something
about God's loving nature and awesome power.

Spend a few minutes looking through the con-
tents of your Bible. How many books or prophets'
names do you recognise? How many Gospels are
there in the New Testament? Read what St John
said about 'The Word' in John 1:1-3.

Fourth Saturday of Lent   *'This Jesus is no ordinary man!'*

Reading   Some of the people who had been listening to Jesus preaching said, 'Surely this man is a prophet?' Others believed that he was the saviour that God had promised to send. The people were confused because the Scriptures foretold that the Messiah would come from Bethlehem, and yet they believed that Jesus came from Nazareth in Galilee.

The chief priests and Pharisees sent some temple guards to arrest Jesus, but when the guards returned empty-handed they demanded angrily, 'Why have you not arrested Jesus?'

'Because this Jesus is no ordinary man!' they replied. 'We have listened to him preaching, and been amazed by everything he has said!'

The Pharisees were furious that so many of the people chose to believe in Jesus, even when they told them not to.

(Based on John 7:40-52)

Daily thought   Few who listened to Jesus speaking about forgiveness and love could fail to be moved and amazed by his compassion and goodness. He did not look at people's guilt or wrong-doings, but believed in their goodness and offered them a new beginning. He took pity on the sick and crippled, he raised the dead to life and became the friend of everyone whose life he touched. He did not judge people by their appearance or position in life, but looked for the goodness in their hearts.

Prayer

Lord,
fill me with your compassion and love,
so that I can see the goodness in others
and not their faults.
Make me grow more and more like you
every day of my life.

Resolution

Ask yourself, 'Would I be recognised by other people as a follower of Christ?' See how many things you can write in your diary which show others that you are a Christian.

Fifth Sunday of Lent
Lazarus comes back to life

Reading

Lazarus and his two sisters, Martha and Mary, were very good friends of Jesus. They lived in a town called Bethany, not far from Jerusalem, and Jesus often went to visit them. One day the sisters sent an urgent message to Jesus because Lazarus was very ill and close to death. Two days later Jesus and his disciples set off for Bethany, but when they arrived they found that Lazarus was dead and had already been buried for four days.

Martha ran to meet Jesus and said to him, 'Lord, if you had been here you could have saved our brother.'

Jesus turned to her and said, 'Your brother will live again. Anyone who believes in me will have eternal life, and he will never die. Do you believe this?'

Martha answered him, 'Yes, Lord, because I know that you are the Son of God.'

When Jesus saw the great sadness of Martha and Mary, he was filled with love. 'Show me where he is buried,' he said.

So they took him to the tomb, where Jesus said to them, 'Roll away the stone, and you will see God's glory.'

They did as he said, and looking up to heaven Jesus prayed. 'Father I thank you, for I know that you always listen to me. Let these people see and believe.' Then he called out in a loud voice, 'Lazarus, get up and come out!'

To everyone's amazement Lazarus appeared, still wrapped in burial cloths, and walked from the tomb. Many people saw what happened that day, and they believed in Jesus.
(Based on John 11:1-44)

Daily thought   God is the giver of life, and Jesus wants us to understand that death is not the end, but the beginning of eternal life. Jesus helped Martha to understand that he was the 'resurrection and the life', and anyone who believed in him will be raised up after death to join God in everlasting glory.

Prayer   Lord, help me to be like Martha,
  to see clearly that you are the son of God
  and the life of the world.
Make my belief
  and your life in me
  grow a little stronger day by day.

Resolution   In your diary list the names of people close to you who have died, and say a special prayer remembering them.

Fifth Monday of Lent   *Jesus forgives a woman*

Reading   Jesus was teaching in the Temple when the Pharisees brought a woman to stand before him. 'This woman has been caught doing something wrong, and the law says that she should be stoned. What do you think?' they asked, because they wanted to trick Jesus.

After a few moments Jesus stood up and said, 'Let the person who has never done anything wrong throw the first stone at her.'

The crowd that had gathered began to leave one by one, until Jesus and the woman stood alone. Jesus asked her, 'Has anyone thrown a stone at you?'

'No, sir,' she answered.

'Then I have forgiven you,' he said. 'Now go and make a fresh start.'
(Based on John 8:1-11)

Daily thought   Just as in the time of Jesus, people today are only too ready to accuse others and expose their guilt and shame. The newspapers delight in sharing such sad stories.

Jesus did not judge the woman. Instead he treated her with compassion and understanding, and was ready to give her the chance to start afresh. When we admit our mistakes, Jesus forgives our sins and allows us to look to the future. No one except God is perfect, and when we find faults in other people, we must remember that we have our own faults too!

Prayer   Merciful Jesus,
    help me to be understanding and forgiving,
    and to remember
    that we all make mistakes sometimes.

Resolution   All too often we are like the people in the crowd –
quick to judge others without recognising our
own faults. Try this!

A Imagine you are the woman Jesus forgave.
Write some words which describe how you feel
when you hear what Jesus says to you.

B Now imagine you are one of the crowd holding
a stone in your hand. How do those same
words of Jesus make you feel? Write your ideas
down and compare the two sets of answers.

Fifth Tuesday of Lent   *Like Father, like Son*

Reading   While preaching in the temple, Jesus said to the people, 'I am going away, but you cannot come with me, because I do not belong to this world.'

The people were puzzled by this, and asked Jesus, 'Who are you?'

So Jesus answered, 'When you have lifted up the Son of God, then you will know who I am. Everything I teach you has been taught to me by my Father, who is forever with me and I do whatever pleases him.'

Many who listened to Jesus that day believed in him.

(Based on John 8:20-25, 28-30)

Daily thought   'Like father, like son' is a saying which people use when a son has particular characteristics or a personality which is very similar to his father's. We can certainly use this expression when we talk about Jesus, because Jesus is one with his heavenly Father. The God of the Old Testament was awesome and sometimes frightening, and people believed that no one could even look on his 'face' and live! Jesus taught us to call God 'our Father', and reveals God to us as someone who is forgiving, patient and full of unending love for each one of us.

Prayer   Say the Lord's Prayer slowly, thinking about the meaning of the words.

Resolution   If someone asked you to 'describe' God, what would you tell them? Such a simple question is not easy to answer! Try to remember what Jesus tells us about our heavenly Father, and see if you can write down some words you feel describe him.

Fifth Wednesday of Lent   *Keep the faith*

Reading   Nebuchadnezzar, king of Babylon, gave orders for a huge golden statue to be built, and commanded all his people to worship this statue. Three friends called Shadrach, Meshach and Abednego refused to obey the king, and were summoned before him.

'If you don't worship my statue, I will have you thrown into a fiery furnace!' said the king angrily.

The three friends replied, 'We only worship one true God and we will not worship your statue. We are not afraid, because we know our God will protect us.'

King Nebuchadnezzar was so furious he ordered the furnace to be made even hotter than usual. The three friends were bound with rope and thrown into the fiery furnace.

The king watched in amazement as the three young men stood unharmed in the fire, as a mysterious fourth person appeared beside them.

King Nebuchadnezzar exclaimed, 'Shadrach, Meshach and Abednego, come out of the fire!'

The three friends stepped from the fire and to everyone's amazement, not so much as a hair on their heads had been singed.

The king then declared, 'From this day on, you may worship your God, and my people will worship him too. He sent an angel to cool the furnace and to save you, because you trusted him and were ready to die for his sake.'

(Based on Daniel 3:14-20, 24-25, 28)

Daily thought   The book of Daniel is believed to have been written about 165 BC at a time when the Jews were being cruelly persecuted by King Antiochus. This story of the three brave friends encouraged the Jews to remain faithful to God at all times, and reminded them that God would love and protect such faithfulness and trust. Christians today face many challenges to their faith, and are constantly surrounded by false truths and promises. Daily we are confronted by false 'gods', such as money and material possessions. Being a disciple of Jesus means seeing the world differently, and not putting too much importance on materialistic things. We should remember that when we remain faithful to him, God will take care of us and provide for all our needs.

Prayer

Lord Jesus,
    make my trust in your goodness
    grow stronger each day,
    so that my faith will turn me away
    from any temptation
    which could lead me from your love.

Resolution

Read another Old Testament story about a test of faith in Daniel 6:17-24. Then briefly, in your own words, tell your diary what happens.

Fifth Thursday of Lent   *Jesus is the Son of God*

Reading   Jesus told the crowd, 'Whoever keeps my word and follows my way will live for ever.'

The crowd jeered and said, 'Now we know you are mad! Even Abraham and the prophets had to die! Surely you are not greater than them!'

Jesus answered, 'My glory comes from the Father, the one you call God, although you do not know him as I know him!'

The people grew angry with Jesus and many turned against him.
(Based on John 8:51-59)

Daily thought   The people were angry with Jesus because they believed that he was being disrespectful, when he spoke of God's glory as his own. Jesus was trying to make them see and understand that *he was* the Son of God, but they would not believe him because their hearts were closed. Even when they heard his marvellous teaching and explanation of the Scriptures, or saw him performing miracles, they still did not recognise the glory of God's Son.

Earlier in Lent we heard how some of the disciples caught a glimpse of God's glory when Jesus was transfigured on the mountain top (see page 20). We must learn to look for and see his glory reflected in the people and world around us.

Prayer   Father,
    open my heart to the glory of your Son.
Help me to live his message of love,
    so that I can share his glory and everlasting life.

Resolution   Spend a few minutes writing down some of the things which you see in the world around you which remind you of God's glory.

Fifth Friday of Lent   *Look on the good side*

Reading   An angry crowd of people gathered to stone Jesus and he asked them, 'Why do you wish to harm me when I have only acted with love, as my Father wanted me to do?'

'Because you dare to call yourself the Son of God!' they answered.

'Anyone who has seen my works will know that God the Father is in me, and I am in him,' Jesus replied.

Some of the people in the crowd said to one another, 'This man is indeed as special as John the Baptist promised he would be!' and they believed in him.

(Based on John 10:31-42)

Daily thought Take a look at the picture. What do you see? Some people see a vase and others see two faces! It seems strange that two people can look at the same thing and yet see something completely different. Many people listened to Jesus preaching and saw the miracles he performed, but only some saw that he was the Son of God. Sometimes the outward appearance and actions of people can be misleading and we are too quick to judge them on first impressions. We must learn, with God's help, to look into people's hearts and see what is inside to know whether they are filled with God's goodness.

Prayer   Father, pour your goodness into my heart.
              Help me not to judge others
                  by their appearance or on first impressions,
                  but always to look for your goodness
                  and love inside them.

Resolution Write down one positive thing about someone you
                dislike, and in future, difficult though it might be,
                try to see God's goodness in them!

Fifth Saturday of Lent   *'Jesus must be killed!'*

Reading   Some of the people who had seen Jesus raise
Lazarus from the dead went to the Pharisees and
told them what he had done! The Pharisees and
chief priests were afraid that more and more of
the people would believe that Jesus was the
Saviour that God had promised to send.

'They will make him their leader and cause
trouble with the Romans who will punish all of
us,' they said.

Then Caiaphas, the High Priest, spoke. 'Surely it
is better to destroy one man than allow a whole
people to be destroyed.'

So the leaders of the people began plotting how
to kill Jesus.

(Based on John 11:45-53)

Daily thought   Over the past five weeks we have been making a
Lenten journey with Jesus, getting to know him –
and ourselves – better on the way. He has shown
us a God who is loving and forgiving, who takes
care of his people and wants to share everlasting
happiness with us. The power of Jesus' leadership
came from love, not from force or fear, and the
Pharisees were afraid because they knew that
they could never compete. There are countries in
the world today where leaders rule by fear and
threats, and imprison or punish anyone who
threatens their authority. People who are filled
with God's spirit stand up for the rights of the
poor and demonstrate against dishonesty and
corruption, and many are persecuted or killed for
the sake of their love.

Prayer   Dear Lord,
          help me to remember the people today
          who lead with love and suffer persecution
          because others feel threatened by their power.
          Like Jesus, may they stand up for what is right
          and be true to you, our heavenly Father.

Resolution   Think about children who live where there is fear
          and terror. If you could send them a gift to show
          that you cared, what would you send, and why?
          Could you make a donation to a charity which
          helps children in need?

68

Palm Sunday   *Jesus rides into Jerusalem*

Reading   Jesus and his disciples arrived at the Mount of
Olives just outside Jerusalem. He sent two of the
disciples to the next village to collect a donkey
and her foal. 'If anyone stops you, tell them that
they are for me,' he said.

They brought the animals to Jesus, and put
cloaks on their backs so that Jesus could ride on
them. When the people heard that Jesus was coming they laid their cloaks on the road before him,
and pulled branches off the palm trees to wave in
the air.

The crowds grew more and more excited and
shouted at the top of their voices, 'Hosanna,
Hosanna! Blessed is the one sent by the Lord.'

Excitement filled the whole city, and some people
asked, 'Who is this man?'

The people answered them, ' It is Jesus from
Nazareth in Galilee.'
(Based on Matthew 21:1-11)

Daily thought   Jesus rode into Jerusalem as a King of peace and
love, riding on a meek and humble donkey. The
crowds welcomed him as their Saviour, yet only
days later, their cries of 'Hosanna' would change
to 'Crucify him!' Jesus knew that he would be
handed over to suffer and die, when the only
thing he was guilty of was love. He was always
obedient to his Father's will, even to accepting
death on the cross. Would we be so brave if our
obedience to God was put to the test?

Prayer

Lord Jesus,
  Prince of Peace,
  I pray that your peace will spread
  throughout our world today
  and touch the lives of people everywhere.

Resolution

Imagine the scene as Jesus rode into Jerusalem, and describe it in your diary.

Monday of Holy Week   *Mary's gift to Jesus*

Reading   Just before the Passover Feast, Jesus went to visit Martha and Mary and their brother Lazarus. After sharing a meal together, Mary poured expensive ointment over the feet of Jesus and wiped it away with her long hair.

The disciple called Judas said angrily, 'This precious ointment could have been sold, and the money given to the poor instead of being wasted like this!'

Jesus said to Judas, 'Leave her alone! Mary has chosen wisely. You will always have the poor with you, but you will not always have me.'
(Based on John 12:1-8)

Daily thought   Have you ever had an extravagant treat – taken somewhere or bought something special? Most of us have experienced such an expression of love and generosity at some time. Mary wanted to show Jesus just how much she loved him, and how grateful she was for her brother's life (see page 56). She did not worry about the cost of the ointment, and used her own hair to dry Jesus' feet. Her extravagant actions spoke louder than words could ever do, and Jesus must have been deeply touched by her love.

Prayer   Lord Jesus,
       how many times
       have I taken your love for granted?
How many times have I accepted your gifts,
       and forgotten to even say thank you?
I thank you now for all these things,
       and for dying on the cross for me.

Resolution   Think of an extravagant gesture you could make to show someone how much you care about them! Write down your ideas – it could be buying flowers or chocolates with your pocket money, or bringing someone breakfast in bed! Tell your diary later how much your gesture was appreciated!

Tuesday of Holy Week   *Peter lets Jesus down*

Reading   As Jesus shared the Passover meal with his twelve
closest friends he told them, 'One of you will make
me very sad tonight!'
The disciples were dismayed at his words.
'Surely you are mistaken, Lord!'
But he answered, 'One of you sharing this very
meal will hand me over to my enemies!'
'Lord, who will it be?' they asked.
'Whoever shares this bread with me,' he said,
just as Judas Iscariot reached across and took a
piece of bread from the same dish.
Then Jesus explained to his disciples that he
would not be with them for much longer, and that
they could not follow where he was going.
Peter said to him, 'Lord, I am ready to die for
your sake!'
But Jesus told him that before the cock had
crowed that same night, Peter would deny him
three times.
(Based on John 13:21-33, 36-38)

Daily thought   Peter was always eager to make rash promises and
to act on the spur of the moment! He thought that
he was ready to make the ultimate sacrifice and lay
down his own life for the sake of his master whom
he loved and admired. Sometimes we too make
promises only to find, as Peter did, that we cannot
keep them because we are afraid. We might fear
what other people will think or say, and our
courage might fail us because we are unsure of
what the future holds. Even though Peter let Jesus
down when he needed his friendship most, Jesus
forgave him. Such forgiveness and love gave Peter
the strength and courage to do what Jesus asked.

Prayer

Lord Jesus,
Peter denied you three times
but you forgave him.
I ask for your forgiveness
for the times I have turned away
from your friendship and love.

Resolution

Have you ever let someone down? How did it make you feel? In your diary describe how you think Peter might have felt after denying Jesus three times.

Wednesday of Holy Week   *The Last Supper*

Reading   As Jesus and his disciples were eating the Passover meal together, Jesus took some bread and said a prayer of blessing. He broke the bread and gave it to them, saying, 'Take this and eat it, this is my body.'

Then he took a cup of wine and said a prayer of thanks. He passed the cup to each of them and said, 'Take this and drink it, for this is my blood. Just as my Father promised, it will be poured out to save you from your sins.'

(Based on Matthew 26:26-29)

Daily thought   The Passover meal is a celebration to mark the Israelites' escape from slavery in Egypt in Old Testament times. God had made a covenant, or promise, to free his people from slavery. Through the bread and wine at the Last Supper Jesus made a new covenant, a promise to free us from the slavery of sin. In the Eucharistic bread and wine Jesus gives up his body and sheds his blood to offer us new and everlasting life.

Prayer   Lord Jesus,
                         you gave your life for me out of love.
                     Help me to share that love
                         you poured out so generously
                         with everyone I meet.

Resolution   Draw a picture of the Last Supper scene. Remember to include the bread and wine which Jesus shared in such a special way at this last meal with his disciples.

Maundy Thursday   *Jesus washes the disciples' feet*

Maundy Thursday is the Thursday before Easter. The word 'Maundy' comes from the Latin word 'mandatum' meaning commandment, and refers to John 13:34 where Jesus gives a new commandment to 'love one another as I have loved you'.

Reading

Knowing that the time had come for him to return to his heavenly Father, Jesus and his disciples gathered to celebrate one last Passover meal together.

Getting up from the table, he poured some water into a basin and, wrapping a towel around his waist, began to wash the feet of his disciples. When it was Peter's turn he tried to stop Jesus by saying, 'Lord, it is not right that you should be washing my feet.'

But Jesus said to all of them, 'I, your Lord and Master, have washed your feet. I have shown you how it should be, so that you will go away and wash each other's feet.'

(Based on John 13:1-16)

Daily thought

Even at a time when Jesus was preparing to suffer and die on the cross, he didn't think of himself but was ready as always to put the needs of others first. Before he left his disciples he wanted to give them a final message, and his action of washing their feet spoke louder than words. As disciples of Jesus we are called to 'serve' one another, to act with humility and love, and to treat everyone equally. Jesus showed us the way, and we are asked to follow.

Prayer

Jesus, Son of God and friend to all,
   out of love for us
   you humbled yourself to become man
   and to die on the cross.
Help me to be humble
   and to be ready to serve others
   and to think of their needs before my own.

Resolution

Jesus showed us how to serve one another, so think of a 'service' you could do for someone else. It might be as simple as doing the washing-up or cleaning the car. Tell your diary what you decide to do.

Good Friday

Jesus is put to death

Reading   Jesus was taken before Caiaphas, the High Priest, and the elders. They decided that Jesus should be put to death, and they sent him to be sentenced by the Roman governor, Pontius Pilate. Pilate was afraid that the crowds would cause trouble, so he agreed to crucify Jesus knowing that he had done nothing wrong. The Roman soldiers made fun of Jesus by making a crown of thorns for the 'King of the Jews'. Then they beat him and forced him to carry his own cross. After Jesus had stumbled and fallen several times, the soldiers ordered a man called Simon to help him.

When they got to Golgotha (a name which means 'the place of the skull'), they nailed Jesus to the cross and wrote above him, 'This is Jesus, King of the Jews.'

Two thieves were crucified next to Jesus, and they joined the crowd in mocking Jesus and his claim to be God's Son. 'He saved others, but he can't save himself!' they jeered.

After hanging on the cross for many hours, Jesus called out in a loud voice, 'Father why have you deserted me!' and then he died.
(Based on Matthew 26:57, 65; 27:1-2, 23-50)

Daily thought   If the story of Jesus had ended on Good Friday with his death on the cross, then indeed it would be a very sad story. Certainly for his disciples, Mary his mother and his many faithful followers and friends, the events of Good Friday must have been unbearably sad and disappointing. Knowing that death on the cross is not the end, but only the beginning, allows us to look ahead with hope and expectation. Jesus suffered and died out of love for us, before rising from the dead, just as we will, to share everlasting life with God our Father in heaven.

Prayer

Lord Jesus,
as I think about your suffering and death,
help me to remember those in the world
who are suffering and dying every day.
May they find comfort in the knowledge
that your death has allowed each one of us
to share in the glory of your resurrection
and life everlasting.

Resolution

Try to imagine the Crucifixion scene – the three crosses, the soldiers, the crowd, Mary the mother of Jesus, and his followers. Describe the scene in your diary.

Holy Saturday   *A day of waiting*

Reading   I will praise you, Lord,
      because you have saved me.
You have rescued my soul from death
and given me back my life.

I will sing songs of thanks to the Lord,
and show the depth of my love for him.
His goodness lasts for ever.
He wipes away my tears,
      and fills my life with happiness.

The Lord is merciful and comes to my aid.
He changes my sadness into joy
and I will give thanks for ever
      to the Lord my God.
(Based on Psalm 29/30:1, 3-5, 10-12)

Daily thought   After the busy events of Holy Week and the sadness of Jesus' suffering and death on Good Friday, Holy Saturday is a day of waiting, when the church lies quiet and bare. This is a day filled with mystery and amazement as we wait with eager anticipation to celebrate the resurrection of Jesus and his victory over death. Tomorrow we will rejoice and give thanks and praise to God for sending his only Son to save us from death and giving us the gift of eternal life.

Prayer   Lord Jesus,
      help me to remember
      that you suffered and died on the cross for me,
      so that I too can share the joy
      of everlasting life with you.

Resolution   As Lent comes to an end, look back through your diary and see how many different things you have achieved. Which days were rewarding, and which did you struggle with? Write down any ideas or suggestions you might have for next year's Lenten journey!

Easter Sunday   *Alleluia! Jesus is risen!*

Reading   Before sunrise on the Sunday morning, Mary of
                     Magdala went to the tomb. As she reached the
                     entrance, she saw that the stone had been rolled
                     away and the tomb was empty. She ran to the dis-
                     ciples saying, 'They have taken the Lord from the
                     tomb and we don't know where they have put him!'
                        Peter and another disciple, John, ran to the tomb
                     and found it just as Mary had described, with the
                     linen burial cloths lying on the ground. Peter went
                     into the tomb first, and then John followed him.
                     Until this moment they had not understood the
                     Scriptures which said, 'He must rise from the
                     dead,' but now they saw, and they believed.
                     (Based on John 20:1-9)

Daily thought   Today we celebrate that Jesus has risen from the
                     dead and is alive today! Our God is here with us
                     now, in you and me and the people all around us.
                     On our journey through Lent we have learned
                     what sort of people Jesus calls us to be, and the path
                     which we must follow not only in Lent, but *every
                     day* if we are to share everlasting life with him.

Prayer   Alleluia, alleluia,
                        Jesus is risen from the dead.
                     Rejoice and be glad,
                        alleluia

Resolution   Although Lent has come to an end, think about
                     how you can put your resolutions into practice in
                     your daily life.

Diary

Ash Wednesday   *God will see your goodness*

_____

_____

_____

_____

_____

_____

_____

Thursday after Ash Wednesday   *'Follow me'*

_____

_____

_____

_____

_____

_____

_____

Friday after Ash Wednesday   *Know what is important*

_____

_____

_____

_____

_____

_____

_____

86

Saturday after Ash Wednesday   *Turn over a new leaf*

_____
_____
_____
_____
_____
_____
_____

First Sunday of Lent   *Don't be tempted*

_____
_____
_____
_____
_____
_____
_____

First Monday of Lent   *Treat others well*

_____
_____
_____
_____
_____
_____
_____

First Tuesday of Lent   *Make time for God*

_____

_____

_____

_____

_____

_____

_____

First Wednesday of Lent   *Making choices*

_____

_____

_____

_____

_____

_____

_____

First Thursday of Lent   *God knows best*

_____

_____

_____

_____

_____

_____

_____

88

First Friday of Lent   *Make peace*

_____
_____
_____
_____
_____
_____
_____

First Saturday of Lent   *Love everyone*

_____
_____
_____
_____
_____
_____
_____

Second Sunday of Lent   *God's glory*

_____
_____
_____
_____
_____
_____
_____

Second Monday of Lent *Be fair*

_____
_____
_____
_____
_____
_____
_____

Second Tuesday of Lent *Practise what you preach*

_____
_____
_____
_____
_____
_____

Second Wednesday of Lent *A place in heaven*

_____
_____
_____
_____
_____
_____

Second Thursday of Lent　　　*Lazarus and the rich man*

_____
_____
_____
_____
_____
_____
_____

Second Friday of Lent　　　*Listen to God's message*

_____
_____
_____
_____
_____
_____
_____

Second Saturday of Lent　　　*The son who came back*

_____
_____
_____
_____
_____
_____
_____

Third Sunday of Lent *The water of life*

_____
_____
_____
_____
_____
_____
_____

Third Monday of Lent *The power of God's word*

_____
_____
_____
_____
_____
_____
_____

Third Tuesday of Lent *Keep on forgiving*

_____
_____
_____
_____
_____
_____
_____

Third Wednesday of Lent   *God's rules*

Third Thursday of Lent   *Listen to God's call*

Third Friday of Lent   *The greatest Commandments*

Third Saturday of Lent   *The Pharisee and the tax-collector*

_____

_____

_____

_____

_____

_____

Fourth Sunday of Lent   *The Light of the World*

_____

_____

_____

_____

_____

_____

Fourth Monday of Lent   *Have faith*

_____

_____

_____

_____

_____

_____

Fourth Tuesday of Lent *The paralysed man*

_____

_____

_____

_____

_____

_____

_____

Fourth Wednesday of Lent *'Believe in me and
the one who sent me'*

_____

_____

_____

_____

_____

_____

_____

Fourth Thursday of Lent *'I have the message of eternal life'*

_____

_____

_____

_____

_____

_____

Fourth Friday of Lent   *'I come from the one who sent me'*

_____
_____
_____
_____
_____
_____

Fourth Saturday of Lent   *'This Jesus is no ordinary man!'*

_____
_____
_____
_____
_____
_____

Fifth Sunday of Lent   *Lazarus comes back to life*

_____
_____
_____
_____
_____
_____

Fifth Monday of Lent

Jesus forgives a woman

Fifth Tuesday of Lent

Like Father, like Son

Fifth Wednesday of Lent

Keep the faith

Fifth Thursday of Lent   *Jesus is the Son of God*

_____
_____
_____
_____
_____
_____
_____

Fifth Friday of Lent   *Look on the good side*

_____
_____
_____
_____
_____
_____
_____

Fifth Saturday of Lent   *'Jesus must be killed!'*

_____
_____
_____
_____
_____
_____
_____

98

Palm Sunday   *Jesus rides into Jerusalem*

_____
_____
_____
_____
_____
_____
_____

Monday of Holy Week   *Mary's gift to Jesus*

_____
_____
_____
_____
_____
_____
_____

Tuesday of Holy Week   *Peter lets Jesus down*

_____
_____
_____
_____
_____
_____

Wednesday of Holy Week

The Last Supper

Maundy Thursday   *Jesus washes the disciples' feet*

_____

_____

_____

_____

_____

_____

_____

Good Friday   *Jesus is put to death*

_____

_____

_____

_____

_____

_____

_____

Holy Saturday   *A day of waiting*

_____

_____

_____

_____

_____

_____

_____

Easter Sunday   *Alleluia! Jesus is risen!*

_____

_____

_____

_____

_____

_____

_____